THE AI INCOME PLAYBOOK

By LeSean Thomas

TABLE OF CONTENTS

DEDICATION

This book is dedicated to everyone who ever asked me, "How did you finally make it?"

To the friends, family members, coworkers, and strangers who watched the journey from the outside and only saw the result, not the process.

To those who wondered how ordinary effort became an extraordinary opportunity.

The truth is, there was no shortcut.

There were systems.
There was discipline.
There was consistency.
There were mistakes.
There were lessons.
There were years of building in silence.

There were mornings when motivation was gone, But commitment remained.

There were moments when quitting felt easier, But the purpose was stronger.

This book is my answer.

It is for those who want more than luck. More than trends. More than temporary success.

It is for those who are ready to build with patience, integrity, and ownership.

If you ever wondered how it happened, it happened one system, one decision, and one disciplined day at a time.

This is for you.

LeSean Thomas

ACKNOWLEDGMENTS

No meaningful work is built alone.

This book exists because of the people who supported me, challenged me, encouraged me, and believed in me during seasons when progress was invisible.

I am deeply grateful to my family and friends who showed patience while I worked quietly and stayed focused on building something lasting.

To the mentors, teachers, authors, and thinkers whose ideas shaped my understanding of discipline, systems, and leadership, thank you for sharing your wisdom.

To every reader who believes in personal growth, integrity, and ownership, this work is for you.

And to everyone who questioned the journey, doubted the process, or underestimated the vision, thank you as well. You strengthened my resolve.

Nothing worthwhile is built in isolation.

This book is proof of that.

LeSean Thomas

INTRODUCTION

Why This Book Exists

Most people do not fail because they lack intelligence, creativity, or effort. They fail because they lack systems. They work hard, learn constantly, and stay busy, yet year after year their circumstances barely change. Over time, this creates frustration, doubt, and quiet resignation.

I know this pattern because I lived it.

For years, I believed success came from pushing harder. I thought if I sacrificed more, learned more, and worked longer, something would eventually break through. Sometimes it did. Most of the time, it did not. Progress felt inconsistent. Stability felt fragile. Confidence rose and fell with circumstances.

Everything changed when I stopped trying to "work harder" and started learning how to build systems.

Artificial intelligence did not make me successful. Structure did.

AI simply multiplied it.

This book exists to show you how to design income, stability, and freedom deliberately. Not through hype. Not through shortcuts. Not through empty promises. Through disciplined thinking, ethical systems, and consistent execution.

What follows is not theory. It is a blueprint.

CHAPTER 1
The System Economy and Your Place in It

For most of modern history, success followed a predictable path. People went to school, earned credentials, found employment, and worked long enough to secure stability. This model was not perfect, but it provided direction. It gave people a roadmap.

That roadmap no longer exists.

Over decades, automation, globalization, and digital infrastructure quietly dismantled it. Companies learned how to outsource. Software replaced departments. Algorithms replaced managers. Entire industries transformed or disappeared. Stability became temporary. Careers became contracts.

Most people did not notice when this happened. They simply felt the effects later. Jobs became harder to keep. Income became unpredictable. Stress increased. Planning became difficult.

At the same time, power shifted.

For the first time in history, individuals gained access to tools once reserved for corporations. Cloud platforms, artificial intelligence, global payment systems, and digital distribution networks became available to anyone with discipline and internet access.

One person could now operate like a company.

But only if they knew how.

Most did not.

They kept using new tools with old thinking.

They stayed trapped in reaction mode.

They worked inside systems designed by others.

They rented an opportunity.

System builders own it.

Modern success belongs to those who design infrastructure rather than simply performing tasks. Infrastructure includes processes, workflows, platforms, and networks. When you control infrastructure, you control value creation. When you do not, you remain dependent.

Michael learned this after losing his engineering position during a corporate restructuring. Despite strong performance and loyalty, his role was automated. Income dropped suddenly. Confidence suffered. He rebuilt by creating consulting systems, digital products, and automated services. He never depended on one employer again.

The lesson was clear.

Effort without architecture fails.

Architecture without effort stagnates.

You need both.

Your responsibility in the modern economy is to build personal ecosystems: multiple income streams, diversified platforms, adaptable skills, and owned assets. When one weakens, others compensate. This is resilience.

This is freedom.

Before moving forward, ask yourself honestly where your income comes from, what systems support it, and what would happen if one collapsed. Your answers determine your future.

CHAPTER 2
The Digital Command Center

Before you can build a stable income, authority, or freedom, you must first build order. Most people underestimate this step. They believe success begins with ideas, motivation, or talent. In reality, it begins with the environment. Your environment shapes how you think, how you act, and how effectively you execute.

In the digital age, your primary environment is not an office or a building. It is your laptop, your phone, your cloud storage, your applications, and your communication systems. This is where nearly all modern work happens. Whether you realize it or not, this digital environment either supports your growth or sabotages it.

When your systems are chaotic, your life becomes chaotic.

When your systems are structured, your life becomes structured.

Most people operate in a silent disorder. Files are scattered. Notes are incomplete. Passwords are forgotten. Calendars conflict. Important information is buried in messages or lost entirely. Each individual problem feels small. Together, they create constant friction. Over time, this friction drains energy and confidence.

People often interpret this exhaustion as personal weakness.

It is not.

It is an environmental failure.

Sophia learned this after years of running an online coaching business. From the outside, she appeared successful. Internally, she was overwhelmed. Client information lived on multiple platforms. Payment records were inconsistent. Project timelines were unclear. She worked constantly and still felt behind. One weekend, she rebuilt her systems from scratch. She centralized storage, standardized naming, integrated tools, and created dashboards. Within weeks, her stress decreased. Within months, her income increased. Nothing about her talent changed. Her structure did.

Order is not about perfection. It is about accessibility. It means knowing where things are. It means being able to act without hesitation. It means removing unnecessary obstacles between intention and execution.

Every serious builder maintains one central system: a command center. This is the primary location where strategy, documentation, planning, and oversight occur. It is the source of truth. When information is scattered across multiple unconnected platforms, confusion is inevitable. Centralization creates clarity.

Designing your command center begins with simple architecture. Organize your digital life into clear categories: strategy, clients, products, marketing, operations, and finance. These pillars reflect the basic functions of any enterprise. Everything you create should belong somewhere within them.

Naming is a leadership skill. Poor naming creates confusion. Clear naming reduces cognitive load. When files, folders, and documents are labeled consistently, your mind is freed for higher-level thinking. You stop searching. You start executing.

A personal knowledge vault is another essential component. Most people forget their own insights. They solve problems, learn lessons, and develop frameworks, only to lose them over time. A knowledge system preserves thinking. It allows wisdom to compound. It becomes a second mind.

Relying on memory is risky. Human memory is emotional and unreliable. It distorts timelines, forgets details, and prioritizes feelings over facts. Systems remember accurately. Professionals document what matters.

Security is part of stewardship. Devices fail. Accounts are compromised. Data is corrupted. Without backups and safeguards, years of work can disappear instantly. Responsible builders implement redundancy, encryption, and access controls. Protecting information is protecting future opportunity.

High performers practice regular system maintenance. Weekly reviews prevent collapse. They clear inboxes, update tasks, archive clutter, and plan ahead. This ritual keeps complexity from accumulating. Discipline at small scales creates freedom at large scales.

Complex systems impress beginners. Simple systems endure. If you cannot explain your workflow clearly, it will eventually fail. Elegance scales. Complexity breaks.

Across cultures and spiritual traditions, order has always been associated with harmony. When life is ordered, energy flows. When it is chaotic, energy leaks. Digital systems are modern expressions of this principle. They reflect respect for time, opportunity, and purpose.

To build your command center, begin with an audit. Delete what no longer matters. Consolidate what remains. Create clear folders. Establish naming rules. Integrate essential tools. Document core processes. Then maintain weekly.

Avoid self-deception. Statements like "I'll organize later" or "I know where everything is" are comfort stories. They delay growth. Structure creates capacity.

Over time, ordered systems reduce stress, increase speed, strengthen confidence, and expand opportunity. They allow you to operate at higher levels without burnout.

Ask yourself honestly: if your primary device disappeared tomorrow, could you recover quickly? If you took a week off, would your work collapse? Your answers reveal what must be built.

CHAPTER 3
Mastering Artificial Intelligence as a Strategic Partner

When artificial intelligence became widely accessible, it was presented as a miracle solution. Headlines promised instant wealth, effortless productivity, and unlimited opportunity. Social media is filled with stories of people claiming overnight success through automated systems. Many believed that effort was about to become obsolete.

This belief was dangerous.

Artificial intelligence did not eliminate the need for thinking. It increased its value. Those who approached AI as a shortcut became dependent and confused. Those who approached it as a tool within structured systems became powerful.

AI is not a replacement for intelligence.

It is a multiplier of it.

Most people who complain that AI is unreliable are actually experiencing leadership failure. They provide vague instructions, limited context, and unclear objectives. Then they blame the tool when results are inconsistent. In reality, AI reflects the quality of direction it receives. Confusion produces confusion.

Professionals treat AI as a junior partner. It is fast, tireless, and capable of processing enormous amounts of information. It also lacks judgment, ethics, and responsibility. Those elements remain human duties. When people abdicate judgment, systems become fragile.

David learned this while working in market research. His reports were thorough but slow. He spent days organizing data, identifying patterns, and writing summaries. After redesigning his workflow, AI handled data parsing, preliminary analysis, and drafting. David focused on interpretation and strategy. His output tripled. His quality improved. His income increased. Systems created leverage.

Understanding how AI operates is essential. AI does not think or understand meaning. It predicts patterns in language and data. It generates responses based on probability. This is why context matters so much. When you provide a clear structure, you guide probability toward usefulness. When you do not, randomness appears.

Effective AI communication follows a pattern. You must define role, objective, environment, constraints, and format. Without these elements, output fluctuates. Over time, advanced users develop prompt libraries. They test variations, refine language, and document successful workflows. These libraries become intellectual property.

True mastery lies in workflow design, not individual prompts. Research, analysis, strategy, production, review, and distribution should each have defined processes. AI supports different stages differently. When these stages are integrated, reliability emerges.

Verification is non-negotiable. AI accelerates creation but does not guarantee accuracy. Facts, calculations, legal claims, and financial advice must be reviewed. Blind trust is negligence. Responsibility cannot be automated.

Ethical boundaries are equally important. Technology amplifies intention. If the intention is dishonest, harm multiplies. Using AI to deceive, impersonate, or steal may produce short-term gains, but it destroys long-term credibility. Reputation is more valuable than any shortcut.

Some users develop psychological dependence on AI. They stop analyzing, questioning, and thinking critically. Their skills deteriorate. AI becomes a crutch. Professionals remain mentally engaged. They collaborate with technology rather than surrender to it.

Mastery requires practice. Elite users experiment deliberately. They analyze failures, refine workflows, and document improvements. Small refinements accumulate into major advantages over time.

Across history, new forms of power have always required wisdom. Those who use power without restraint eventually collapse. Those who combine power with humility thrive. AI is power. Handle it carefully.

To build your personal AI operating system, begin by identifying core tasks. Map workflows. Design prompts. Test outputs. Create checkpoints. Document systems. Review monthly. Over time, this becomes infrastructure.

Common self-sabotage patterns include blind trust, random prompting, lack of documentation, overautomation, and ethical shortcuts. Each leads to failure. Avoid them deliberately.

When AI mastery matures, speed increases, costs decrease, quality improves, and capacity expands. You become harder to replace. You become more adaptable. You gain leverage.

Ask yourself whether you are directing technology or reacting to it. Your answer defines your future.

CHAPTER 4
Building Your First Reliable Income System

Most people believe that money problems are caused by a lack of opportunity. They assume that if they could just find the right job, the right business idea, or the right connection, everything would change. In reality, most financial instability comes from a lack of structure. Income rises and falls not because people are incapable, but because their systems are fragile.

Reliable income is not about getting lucky.

It is about building predictability.

Predictability creates peace of mind. It allows long-term planning. It reduces emotional pressure. It creates space for strategic thinking. Without it, every decision becomes reactive.

In the early stages, many people rely on random hustling. They try freelancing, selling products, offering services, running ads, or joining platforms. Some things work briefly. Most do not. Energy is scattered. Focus is diluted. Progress is inconsistent. The problem is not effort. The problem is a lack of design.

Before automation, before digital products, and before scaling, there is service. Service forces you to solve real problems for real people. It exposes weaknesses. It provides feedback. It builds credibility. It generates cash flow. Skipping this stage leads to fragile businesses.

Marcus learned this while working across multiple gig platforms. He accepted any job he could find: research, design, administration, writing. Income fluctuated wildly. He analyzed his work and noticed that most clients needed customer follow-up systems. He specialized. He built templates. He created onboarding procedures. He standardized delivery. Within months, his income stabilized. Specialization created leverage.

Clients do not buy tasks.

They buy outcomes.

They do not want email management. They want higher retention. They do not want advertisements. They want more customers. They do not want reports. They want clarity. When you frame your services around results, value increases.

Every strong offer answers four questions: who it serves, what problem it solves, how it solves it, and what changes afterward. If any of these are unclear, sales weaken. Clarity builds trust.

Delivery infrastructure is what separates professionals from amateurs. Intake forms, assessment frameworks, templates, review checklists, and support protocols prevent chaos. When delivery is inconsistent, reputation suffers.

Pricing communicates confidence. Chronic underpricing signals doubt. Overpricing without value signals deception. Fair pricing reflects impact. It respects both the provider and client.

Boundaries protect sustainability. Many beginners burn out by accepting unreasonable demands, responding instantly, and ignoring personal limits. This destroys quality. Professional boundaries protect excellence.

Stable income requires acquisition systems. Outreach frameworks, referral programs, content funnels, and partnerships create a predictable flow. Depending on luck is irresponsible.

Artificial intelligence strengthens services by supporting research, documentation, reporting, scheduling, and communication. It multiplies consistency. Human judgment remains central.

To build your first income system, begin by identifying a common problem. Design a solution framework. Build templates. Create onboarding. Set pricing. Launch outreach. Measure results. Improve continuously.

Psychological barriers often interfere with stability. Fear of charging, fear of visibility, fear of rejection, and fear of commitment cause self-sabotage. Systems reduce emotional interference.

Across cultures, fair exchange has always been considered honorable. The value given should match the value received. Exploitation on either side destroys trust. Balanced exchange sustains success.

When income stabilizes, stress decreases, confidence grows, and opportunities expand. Stability is power. It allows you to think beyond survival.

Examine where your income is fragile. Identify what depends entirely on your presence. Standardize what you can. Systemize what repeats. Build deliberately.

CHAPTER 5
Turning Experience Into Scalable Digital Assets

Every person eventually confronts the same limitation: time. No matter how disciplined, talented, or focused you become, there are only twenty-four hours in a day. When income depends entirely on personal availability, growth stops. You may earn well, but you remain constrained. Digital assets exist to break this limit.

Digital assets transform effort into infrastructure.

They allow your knowledge, systems, and experience to work for you repeatedly without requiring constant presence. They turn temporary labor into lasting value.

Many people misunderstand what makes digital products successful. They believe that information itself has value. In reality, information is abundant. Tutorials, articles, and videos are freely available everywhere. What people pay for is not information. They pay for clarity, structure, and guided transformation.

Rachel learned this while working as a freelance accountant. She answered the same questions daily about budgeting, compliance, and tax planning. Over time, she documented her explanations. She created templates and walkthroughs. She built a digital toolkit. Within two years, product revenue exceeded consulting income. Her experience became capital.

High-value knowledge is often invisible to its owner. It feels obvious. It feels normal. It feels simple. These are signals that you possess transferable skills. Ask yourself what people repeatedly ask you for help with. Notice what problems you solve easily. Identify systems you built for yourself. These are potential products.

Professional products are designed for users, not creators. Many failed products reflect what the creator wanted to say rather than what the user needed to learn. User-centered design anticipates confusion, removes friction, and guides progress step by step. It builds confidence and reduces dropout.

Strong digital products follow clear architecture. Orientation introduces the framework. Foundations establish principles. The application demonstrates use. Optimization improves performance. Maintenance sustains results. When users know where they are in the journey, motivation increases.

Perfectionism is a major enemy of progress. Many people delay launching products for years, waiting for ideal conditions. Meanwhile, others release imperfect versions, learn from feedback, and improve. Speed creates learning. Iteration creates excellence.

Pricing shapes behavior. Free products are often neglected. Low-cost products invite experimentation. Premium products invite commitment. Choose pricing that aligns with the depth of transformation offered.

Distribution is as important as creation. Products require pathways: landing pages, email sequences, content bridges, affiliates, and partnerships. Without distribution systems, even excellent products remain invisible.

Customer feedback is a development engine. Questions, complaints, and usage patterns reveal weaknesses. Builders who listen evolve faster than those who defend.

Over time, single products can be expanded into ecosystems. Entry-level tools introduce concepts. Core programs deliver transformation. Advanced systems deepen mastery. Each supports the next. Retention multiplies revenue.

With scale comes responsibility. Clear terms, transparent pricing, accessible support, and ethical marketing preserve trust. Reputation is fragile. Protect it deliberately.

Building your first digital asset begins with documenting your process. Organize lessons. Create templates. Record explanations. Package professionally. Test with users. Improve monthly. Repeat.

When digital assets mature, income stabilizes, time frees, reach expands, and influence deepens. You own infrastructure. You gain leverage.

Ask yourself what knowledge you are wasting by keeping it private. Identify who could benefit from your systems. Begin building.

CHAPTER 6
Building Authority Through Strategic Content

In the modern economy, attention is currency. Before anyone buys from you, hires you, or trusts you, they must first notice you. Before they notice you, they must see something that signals relevance. Before they see relevance, they must encounter consistent value. This entire process is driven by content.

Content is not entertainment.

It is positioning.

Every article, video, post, email, or presentation you create communicates who you are, what you understand, and how seriously you should be taken. Whether intentional or not, your content builds a public identity.

Most beginners treat content as self-expression. They share opinions, daily experiences, and random thoughts. This may attract attention temporarily, but it rarely builds authority. Authority is created when people repeatedly learn something useful from you. It forms when your voice becomes associated with clarity and reliability.

Thomas learned this while attempting to grow his consulting practice. For years, he posted sporadically about his work. Engagement was minimal. After studying successful educators in his field, he redesigned his approach. He began publishing structured insights, case analyses, and practical frameworks.

Within a year, he became a recognized voice. Content transformed his credibility.

Authority content follows three principles: relevance, consistency, and depth. Relevance ensures that material addresses real problems. Consistency builds familiarity. Depth demonstrates competence. When any element is missing, trust weakens.

Relevance requires listening. Builders who pay attention to questions, objections, and frustrations create more effective content. Markets speak constantly. Those who listen grow faster.

Consistency does not mean constant posting. It means predictable presence. Weekly articles. Daily micro-content. Monthly reports. Regular schedules train audiences to expect value. Irregular output erodes momentum.

Depth separates experts from commentators. Superficial advice is easily forgotten. Insightful analysis is remembered. Depth requires preparation, reflection, and experience. It cannot be faked long-term.

Storytelling is a powerful authority tool. People remember narratives more than instructions. Case studies, journeys, failures, and recoveries humanize expertise. They create an emotional connection.

Artificial intelligence can support content creation through research, outlining, editing, and optimization. It increases speed. It reduces friction. It does not replace voice. An authentic perspective remains irreplaceable.

Platform strategy matters. Different platforms reward different behaviors. Long-form builds credibility. Short-form builds reach.

Email builds ownership. Communities build loyalty. Diversification protects visibility.

Many creators sabotage themselves by chasing trends. Viral formats change constantly. Chasing them produces instability. Sustainable authority comes from principles, not popularity.

Content ecosystems outperform isolated posts. A blog supports a newsletter. A podcast supports courses. Social media supports landing pages. Each channel feeds the others. Integration multiplies impact.

Negative feedback is inevitable. Authority attracts criticism. Professionals respond with composure. They distinguish between useful critique and noise. Emotional reactivity undermines credibility.

Long-term content builders treat creation as infrastructure. Each piece compounds. Over time, libraries form. Libraries create trust at scale. Trust converts to opportunity.

Before leaving this chapter, audit your current public presence. Ask what impression it creates. Determine whether it communicates competence or confusion. Adjust deliberately.

Authority is built sentence by sentence.

Post by post.

Year by year.

CHAPTER 7
Scaling Influence Through Social Systems

Influence has always shaped opportunity. Long before digital platforms existed, reputation, relationships, and community standing determined access to resources and information. In the modern era, social systems have multiplied this effect. A single voice can now reach millions. A single message can shape markets. A single reputation can create or destroy careers.

Influence is not popularity.

It is trust at scale.

Many people chase visibility without understanding this distinction. They seek followers, likes, and impressions. These metrics feel impressive but often translate into little real impact. True influence exists when people act on what you say, when they apply your ideas, when they recommend your work. When they invest in your guidance.

Angela discovered this while building her online fitness brand. Early on, she focused on growing her audience. She followed trends and posted frequently. Her follower count rose, but sales remained low. Eventually, she shifted toward education, personalized engagement, and long-term support. Her audience grew more slowly, but revenue and loyalty increased dramatically. Influence replaced attention.

Social systems are built on relationships. Platforms provide infrastructure, but trust is human. Algorithms amplify signals, but meaning is created through consistency and integrity. Builders who forget this become dependent on trends. Builders who remember it create communities.

Every strong social ecosystem contains three layers: visibility, engagement, and advocacy. Visibility introduces you. Engagement builds connection. Advocacy multiplies reach. Many creators never progress beyond visibility. They remain performers rather than leaders.

Engagement requires responsiveness. When people feel heard, they feel valued. Comments, messages, and feedback are opportunities to deepen relationships. Ignoring them weakens bonds.

Advocacy emerges when value is undeniable. When people benefit consistently, they share voluntarily. Incentives can help, but genuine advocacy is emotional. It is based on appreciation and respect.

Authenticity is central to influence. Audiences are highly sensitive to manipulation. Artificial personas collapse under scrutiny. Sustainable influence requires alignment between private values and public behavior.

AI can assist with scheduling, analysis, moderation, and research. It supports scalability. It does not replace sincerity. Automated engagement without empathy damages trust.

Platform dependence is risky. Algorithms change. Policies shift. Accounts disappear. Wise builders diversify their presence and prioritize owned channels such as email lists and communities. Ownership protects continuity.

Conflict is inevitable in public spaces. Disagreements, misunderstandings, and criticism arise. Professional influence is revealed through response. Calm, respectful communication strengthens reputation. Defensive reactions weaken it.

Social capital compounds. Years of ethical interaction create reservoirs of goodwill. These reservoirs support new initiatives, partnerships, and opportunities. They cannot be built quickly. They require patience.

Leadership in social systems involves moderation and protection. Healthy communities require boundaries. Clear standards prevent toxicity. Without leadership, communities decay.

Spiritual traditions emphasize collective responsibility. Influence carries moral weight. Words shape beliefs. Beliefs shape behavior. Responsible leaders communicate carefully.

Before leaving this chapter, evaluate your social presence. Determine whether it reflects clarity, generosity, and consistency. Ask whether your systems encourage connection or distraction. Adjust accordingly.

Influence is built daily.

One interaction at a time.

CHAPTER 8
Building Micro-Agencies and Retainer Ecosystems

For many independent professionals, there comes a moment when individual effort reaches its limit. No matter how efficient they become, income stops growing. Time becomes scarce. Quality begins to suffer. Stress increases. This is not failure. It is a signal.

It is the signal to build a structure.

Micro-agencies exist to solve this problem. They transform solo operations into coordinated systems. They allow individuals to multiply capacity without sacrificing standards. When designed correctly, they create stability, scalability, and resilience.

Most people misunderstand agencies. They imagine large teams, complex hierarchies, and heavy overhead. In reality, modern micro-agencies are lean. They rely on specialized collaborators, automation, and clear processes. They focus on outcomes rather than bureaucracy.

Daniel learned this while running a successful content marketing business. Demand increased steadily. He tried to handle everything himself. Burnout followed. Deadlines slipped. Clients complained. He realized that personal heroics were unsustainable. He began documenting workflows, training contractors, and standardizing delivery. Within a year, revenue doubled while workload decreased.

The foundation of any agency is repeatability. If work cannot be delivered consistently, delegation fails. Every service must have defined steps, templates, quality standards, and review mechanisms. This transforms creativity into infrastructure.

Retainers are the economic engine of sustainable agencies. Project-based work creates volatility. Retainers create rhythm. They allow clients to budget. They allow providers to plan. Predictability strengthens relationships.

Retainer services must be framed around outcomes, not tasks. Clients do not want hours. They want progress. They want results. They want reliability when retainers are designed around impact, retention increases.

Hiring without systems is a common mistake. New staff amplifies existing weaknesses. Before expanding, leaders must ensure that processes are documented and accessible. Training systems must exist. Performance expectations must be clear.

AI supports agency operations through proposal drafting, reporting, scheduling, research, and documentation. It reduces administrative load. It improves consistency. It does not replace leadership.

Client experience determines longevity. Communication quality, response time, transparency, and empathy influence retention more than technical skill. Relationships sustain businesses.

Pricing must reflect value and sustainability. Underpricing creates resentment. Overpricing without justification destroys trust. Fair pricing supports partnership.

Capacity management protects quality. Overextension leads to mistakes. Professionals set limits. They scale gradually. They protect standards.

Conflict management systems prevent escalation. Clear contracts, communication protocols, and documentation preserve professionalism. Emotion-driven responses destroy relationships.

As agencies mature, leadership becomes central. Leaders must develop others. They must train judgment, not just skills. Organizations rise to the level of their leadership.

Across traditions, collaboration has always been honored. Collective effort magnifies individual contribution. Micro-agencies are modern expressions of this principle.

Before leaving this chapter, assess whether your workload is sustainable. Identify where structure is missing. Consider which tasks could be delegated. Begin building.

CHAPTER 9
Designing Automated Income Systems

Every independent professional eventually encounters the same dilemma: growth increases workload. More clients mean more communication. More products mean more support. More visibility means more requests. Without automation, success becomes exhausting. What was once freedom begins to feel like an obligation.

Automation exists to restore balance.

When designed properly, automated systems allow value to flow without constant supervision. They preserve energy for strategy, creativity, and leadership. They do not eliminate work. They remove unnecessary repetition.

Many people misunderstand automation. They imagine passive income that requires no involvement. This fantasy attracts beginners and disappoints them quickly. Sustainable automation is active infrastructure. It requires design, monitoring, and improvement. It is a living system.

Victor learned this while running an online course platform. Initially, he handled enrollments manually, responded to every inquiry, and issued access individually. Growth made this impossible. Mistakes increased. Customers became frustrated. He rebuilt his operations using automated onboarding, payment processing, and support documentation. Complaints decreased. Retention improved. Revenue stabilized.

Effective automation always begins with clarity. You must understand each step of your value delivery process. Where do customers discover you? How do they decide to buy? How do they receive access? How do they receive support? Where do they encounter friction? Mapping these stages reveals automation opportunities.

Value must precede automation. Systems that automate poor experiences simply accelerate failure. Quality must be established first. Then it can be replicated.

AI plays an important role in automation. It assists with communication, personalization, analysis, and documentation. It enables systems to adapt dynamically. However, it cannot replace accountability. Human oversight remains essential.

Verification safeguards trust. Automated processes occasionally fail. Payments may misprocess. Emails may misfire. Access may malfunction. Professionals monitor systems regularly and maintain rapid response protocols.

Overautomation is dangerous. When human contact disappears entirely, relationships weaken. Strategic touchpoints preserve connection. Balance matters.

Security is integral to automation. Customer data, financial information, and intellectual property must be protected. Breaches destroy credibility. Ethical stewardship requires vigilance.

Scalable systems are modular. They consist of components that can be upgraded independently. When one part fails, the whole does not collapse. This architecture supports resilience.

Data is the nervous system of automation. Conversion rates, engagement metrics, churn rates, and response times reveal health. Without measurement, deterioration goes unnoticed.

Psychological comfort often delays automation. People fear losing control. They prefer familiar chaos to unfamiliar structure. Growth requires overcoming this fear.

Across disciplines, automation has always followed mastery. Tools amplify skill. Without skill, they magnify errors. Builders earn automation through competence.

To begin designing automated income systems, document your current workflow. Identify repetitive tasks. Evaluate tools. Test small systems. Expand gradually. Review monthly.

When automation matures, income stabilizes, stress decreases, and strategic capacity increases. You move from operator to architect.

Ask yourself where your time is being wasted. That is where systems belong.

CHAPTER 10
Building Predictable Client Pipelines

Uncertainty is one of the greatest sources of stress in independent work. When income depends on chance encounters, sporadic referrals, or unpredictable algorithms, confidence fluctuates. Planning becomes difficult. Investment feels risky. Growth feels fragile. Many capable professionals remain trapped in survival mode simply because their opportunity flow is inconsistent.

Predictability changes everything.

When you know that new prospects are entering your ecosystem regularly, your mindset shifts. You stop chasing every opportunity. You stop negotiating from fear. You stop accepting work that does not align with your long-term goals. Stability creates leverage. Leverage creates freedom.

A client pipeline is a structured journey that moves people from awareness to trust to commitment. It is not a list of contacts. It is a system. Without such a system, growth depends on luck. With it, growth becomes deliberate.

Most beginners rely on informal pipelines. They depend on word of mouth, occasional visibility, and personal networks. These sources feel comfortable because they do not require intentional selling. Unfortunately, they are unreliable. Referrals slow. Platforms change. Attention shifts. Income fluctuates.

Professional builders design pathways.

Every strong pipeline begins with discovery. People must first become aware of your existence. This happens through content, partnerships, search visibility, and community engagement. Awareness alone is insufficient. Many people notice and forget. The next stage is education. Prospects must understand what you do, how you work, and why your approach is valuable. Articles, videos, guides, and explanations perform this function.

Education leads to engagement. When people respond to messages, ask questions, or download resources, they signal interest. At this stage, your responsibility is to deepen trust. Transparency, consistency, and proof strengthen confidence. Over time, engagement evolves into evaluation. Prospects compare options. They assess risk. They seek reassurance.

Commitment occurs when confidence outweighs doubt.

Each stage requires support.

Follow-up is a major weakness in most pipelines. Many professionals hesitate to reach out. They fear rejection. They assume disinterest. In reality, most prospects are simply busy. Respectful follow-up often revives momentum. Systems eliminate emotional hesitation.

Customer relationship management tools organize interactions, track progress, and prevent neglect. When communication is systematic, professionalism increases.

AI can enhance pipeline management by analyzing engagement patterns, personalizing messages, and prioritizing leads. Used thoughtfully, it improves attentiveness. Used carelessly, it creates impersonality.

Qualification protects quality. Not every prospect is suitable. Some lack resources. Some lack commitment. Some lack alignment. Early filtering prevents burnout and conflict.

Ethical selling is collaborative. It helps people determine whether your solution fits their situation. When value is genuine, conversations feel supportive rather than manipulative.

Measurement reveals truth. Tracking inquiries, conversions, retention, and feedback exposes weaknesses. Guessing creates blind spots. Data guides improvement.

Diversification protects pipelines. Relying on one platform, one partner, or one channel creates vulnerability. Professionals distribute risk.

Relationships compound. Consistent value builds goodwill. Over time, goodwill becomes opportunity. Trust multiplies.

Before leaving this chapter, examine your current acquisition process. Identify where prospects drop off. Determine where confusion appears. Strengthen weak points.

Predictability is engineered.

CHAPTER 11
Scaling Without Losing Control

Growth is often portrayed as the ultimate measure of success. More clients, more revenue, more visibility, and more recognition are treated as unquestionable signs of progress. Yet behind many impressive numbers are exhausted founders, unstable systems, and fragile organizations. Expansion without structure does not create freedom. It creates pressure.

True scaling is not about becoming bigger.

It is about becoming stronger.

When capacity grows faster than control, problems multiply. Communication breaks down. Quality declines. Financial confusion increases. Decision-making becomes reactive. What once felt empowering becomes overwhelming.

Many promising ventures collapse at this stage.

Not because demand disappears.

Because systems fail.

Isabella experienced this while building her digital marketing firm. After years of steady progress, referrals surged. New clients arrived weekly. Revenue increased dramatically. At first, she felt victorious. Soon, she felt trapped. Deadlines slipped. Teams worked overtime. Clients became frustrated. Mistakes increased. Her reputation began to suffer. She realized that personal effort could not compensate for weak infrastructure.

She paused expansion.

Instead of chasing more contracts, she focused on rebuilding operations. She documented processes, standardized workflows, clarified responsibilities, implemented reporting systems, and created quality controls. For several months, growth slowed. Then stability returned. When she resumed expansion, it was sustainable.

Scaling requires repeatability. Every core process must function reliably regardless of volume. If delivery depends on individual memory, personal heroics, or emotional energy, it cannot scale. Sustainable systems are documented, tested, simplified, and measurable.

Financial systems become critical during growth. Without clear visibility into cash flow, margins, reserves, and obligations, expansion becomes dangerous. Many businesses fail not because they lack customers, but because they mismanage money. Profitability must be monitored continuously.

Delegation is essential. Leaders often resist delegation because they fear loss of control. Others delegate prematurely without structure. Both approaches fail. Effective delegation transfers responsibility through systems. Training materials, performance metrics, and feedback loops enable trust.

AI can support operational management by assisting with scheduling, reporting, analysis, documentation, and customer support. Used thoughtfully, it reduces administrative burden. Used carelessly, it creates blind spots.

Culture becomes increasingly important as organizations grow. Culture is how decisions are made when leaders are absent. If values are undefined, inconsistency spreads. If values are modeled clearly, alignment emerges.

Some entrepreneurs become addicted to growth. They equate expansion with worth. They chase numbers without considering sustainability. This leads to reckless hiring, excessive spending, and poor strategic errors. Mature leaders evaluate growth through resilience.

Scaling brings ethical responsibility. More clients mean more lives influenced. More revenue means more accountability. More visibility means greater impact. Stewardship requires humility.

Healthy growth is deliberate.

It is paced.

It is reviewed.

It is adjusted.

Before leaving this chapter, examine your systems honestly. Identify what depends on constant supervision. Determine what would break if demand doubled. Strengthen foundations.

Strength precedes scale.

CHAPTER 12
Building Resilience and Long-Term Discipline

Every meaningful achievement is built on endurance. Talent may open doors, and opportunity may create momentum, but only resilience determines who remains standing when conditions become difficult. In the long run, success belongs less to the gifted and more to the persistent.

Most people misunderstand discipline. They imagine it as harsh self-control or relentless pressure. In reality, discipline is a form of self-respect. It is the decision to honor commitments even when emotions fluctuate. It is the willingness to act in alignment with long-term goals rather than short-term comfort.

Motivation is unreliable. It rises and falls with sleep, stress, relationships, and circumstances. Those who depend on motivation inevitably stall. Builders design routines that function regardless of mood. They remove decision fatigue. They reduce reliance on willpower. They create environments that support productive behavior.

Progress rarely moves in straight lines. It unfolds in cycles of acceleration, stagnation, regression, and renewal. Beginners interpret slow periods as evidence of failure. Professionals recognize them as natural phases of development. Perspective protects perseverance.

Caleb experienced this while developing his online education platform. During his first year, sales were scarce, and feedback was limited. Friends questioned his commitment. Doubt increased. He considered quitting. Instead, he focused on incremental improvement. He refined lessons, improved user experience, strengthened support, and optimized marketing. In his third year, momentum arrived. Most people quit before this point. He stayed.

Sustainable discipline must be embedded in systems. Relying on personal strength alone is fragile. Schedules, checklists, habit trackers, and accountability structures stabilize performance. When discipline is designed, it becomes automatic.

Physical and mental health are foundational to long-term success. Sleep, nutrition, movement, reflection, and recovery are strategic investments. Exhausted minds make poor decisions. Depleted bodies reduce creativity.

Stress is inevitable. Poor stress management is optional. High performers recognize overload early. They practice emotional regulation, schedule recovery periods, delegate responsibilities, and establish boundaries.

Failure is a teacher. Every setback contains information about system weaknesses. When people interpret failure as personal inadequacy, confidence erodes. When they interpret it as feedback, capability grows.

Small wins matter more than dramatic breakthroughs. Daily progress compounds invisibly. Consistent improvement creates extraordinary transformation.

Most successful individuals maintain personal operating systems. They follow morning routines, weekly reviews, monthly assessments, and annual planning processes. These rituals anchor performance.

Across spiritual traditions, perseverance is honored because difficulty refines character. Endurance strengthens identity. Those who persist grow inwardly as well as outwardly.

Protecting vision is essential. Doubt spreads easily. Comparison weakens resolve. Builders guard their mental environment carefully.

Before leaving this chapter, reflect on how you respond to adversity. Notice whether you adapt or retreat. These patterns shape your future.

Resilience is quiet.

It is daily.

It is decisive.

CHAPTER 13
Building Personal Operating Systems for Excellence

Excellence is rarely the result of extraordinary effort. More often, it is the outcome of ordinary actions performed consistently within well-designed systems. Behind every reliable performer is an invisible architecture that governs how work begins, progresses, and concludes. This architecture is known as a personal operating system.

In professional life, an operating system is not software. It is a structured way of thinking and working. It defines how decisions are made, how priorities are set, how tasks are executed, and how improvement occurs. Without such a system, performance fluctuates. With it, excellence becomes repeatable.

Many people rely on intuition and improvisation. While intuition has value, it is unreliable under pressure. When workloads increase, emotions fluctuate, and deadlines tighten, instinct alone fails. Systems stabilize behavior when conditions become difficult.

Ethan learned this lesson while running his consulting practice. His ideas were respected, but his delivery was inconsistent. Some reports were exceptional. Others were rushed. Clients noticed the variation. Revenue stagnated. He realized that talent without structure was limiting his growth. By documenting his analysis frameworks, standardizing report formats, and creating review protocols, he transformed his practice.

Effective operating systems rest on five foundations: standards, procedures, checkpoints, documentation, and feedback loops. Standards define acceptable quality. Procedures explain how standards are achieved. Checkpoints detect errors early. Documentation preserves knowledge. Feedback loops drive improvement.

Standards remove ambiguity. They answer what "good" looks like. Without standards, quality becomes subjective. Subjectivity creates inconsistency.

Procedures eliminate guesswork. They reduce dependency on memory. They enable repetition.

Checkpoints prevent small mistakes from becoming major failures. Regular reviews protect reputation.

Documentation converts personal knowledge into organizational memory. It enables delegation and continuity.

Feedback loops transform experience into growth. Metrics reveal patterns. Without feedback, stagnation occurs.

Designing your operating system begins with identifying recurring activities. Map workflows. Define triggers, actions, outputs, and reviews. This transforms effort into infrastructure.

Many fear that structure limits creativity. In reality, structure protects it. When routine tasks are systemized, mental space is freed for innovation.

Systems fail when they become too complex, undocumented, or unenforced. Simplicity preserves longevity.

Across traditions, order is associated with harmony. When life is ordered, energy flows efficiently. Operating systems reflect this principle.

Over time, well-designed systems reduce stress, improve quality, strengthen reputation, and expand opportunity.

Before leaving this chapter, identify where an inconsistency appears. Notice where memory replaces structure. These are invitations to build systems.

Excellence is engineered.

CHAPTER 14
Financial Mastery and Wealth Systems

Money influences nearly every major decision in modern life, yet most people are never taught how to manage it systematically. They learn fragments through experience, mistakes, and observation, but rarely through deliberate design. As a result, income increases without stability, success arrives without security, and progress occurs without permanence.

Financial mastery is not about accumulation.

It is about control.

Control over cash flow. Control over obligations. Control over risk. Control over future options. Without control, even high earners remain vulnerable. With control, modest incomes can produce lasting wealth.

Many people confuse earning with prosperity. They focus exclusively on increasing revenue, believing that more money will solve their problems. In reality, unmanaged income amplifies weaknesses. Poor budgeting becomes more expensive. Impulsive spending becomes more damaging. Confusion becomes more dangerous.

Jordan learned this after his consulting business began generating significant revenue. He upgraded his lifestyle quickly. He delayed planning. When market conditions shifted, contracts slowed. Savings were minimal. Stress returned. He rebuilt his approach by implementing structured budgeting, reserves, and automated investments. Stability replaced anxiety.

Financial systems begin with visibility. Every serious builder maintains clear records of income, expenses, liabilities, assets, and obligations. They know where money enters and where it leaves. This clarity prevents denial and enables strategic adjustment.

Cash flow is the heartbeat of any enterprise. Profit on paper means little if payments are delayed and obligations are immediate. Healthy systems prioritize liquidity. Emergency reserves and conservative forecasting protect against volatility.

Budgeting is intentional allocation. It replaces impulse with purpose. When budgets reflect values, money becomes a tool rather than a source of conflict.

Debt requires discernment. Productive debt supports income generation. Consumptive debt finances temporary comfort. Financial maturity lies in distinguishing the two.

Automation strengthens wealth systems. Automated savings, investments, tax provisions, and expense tracking ensure consistency. Systems outperform intentions.

Investment converts surplus into future capacity. Whether through businesses, real estate, or education, investments must align with risk tolerance and time horizon. Speculation disguised as strategy produces instability.

Risk management protects progress. Insurance, diversification, and conservative leverage prevent catastrophic loss.

Ethical clarity matters. Wealth acquired through deception rarely produces peace. Sustainable prosperity aligns with contribution.

As systems mature, fear decreases. Decision-making improves. Money becomes infrastructure rather than obsession.

Before leaving this chapter, examine your financial habits honestly. Identify patterns of avoidance or impulsivity. Structure where chaos exists.

Wealth is constructed deliberately.

CHAPTER 15
Leadership, Influence, and Long-Term Legacy

Every person who builds something meaningful eventually becomes a leader, whether they intend to or not. Leadership does not begin with titles, authority, or public recognition. It begins with responsibility. The moment others are affected by your decisions, your systems, or your words, you are leading.

Many people associate leadership with charisma or dominance. They imagine strong personalities and visible power. In reality, the most effective leaders often work quietly. They focus on clarity, consistency, and character. They influence through reliability rather than force.

Leadership begins internally. Before guiding others, individuals must learn to guide themselves. Self-discipline, ethical standards, emotional regulation, and reflective thinking form the foundation of credibility. Without internal alignment, external influence becomes unstable.

Marcus experienced this transition while managing a growing creative agency. His technical skills were exceptional, but his leadership skills were undeveloped. He avoided difficult conversations and delayed decisions. Over time, morale declined, and productivity weakened. Through mentorship and self-study, he learned to establish expectations, provide feedback, and model accountability. Trust returned.

Influence emerges from consistency. When actions match words, credibility forms. When commitments are honored, trust deepens. When mistakes are acknowledged, respect increases. Over time, reputation becomes an asset.

Communication is central to leadership. Clear communication reduces uncertainty. Ambiguity creates anxiety. Leaders invest in learning how to articulate vision and expectations constructively.

As influence expands, ethical responsibility intensifies. Power amplifies impact. Decisions affect livelihoods and opportunities. Ethical leaders balance ambition with stewardship.

Mentorship multiplies impact. By transferring knowledge and confidence, leaders empower others. Effective mentors develop judgment rather than dependency.

Legacy is built through systems, not symbols. Titles fade. Processes endure. Values persist. Leaders who design resilient systems leave lasting contributions.

Humility preserves influence. No individual sees the full picture. Feedback prevents blind spots. Isolation creates vulnerability.

Financial success amplifies responsibility. Wealth increases the capacity to support communities and innovation. Responsible leaders use resources wisely.

Many traditions emphasize servant leadership. Authority exists to serve. Leaders who adopt this mindset create environments where people thrive.

Pressure reveals character. Shortcuts appear. Compromises tempt. Integrity under pressure defines legacy.

Before leaving this chapter, reflect on how your actions affect others. Consider the culture you are shaping. Influence is never neutral.

Leadership is stewardship.

CHAPTER 16
Integration, Mastery, and the Path Forward

Every meaningful journey reaches a point where learning becomes living. Concepts that once required effort become instinctive. Systems that once demanded attention begin operating quietly in the background. This is the stage where knowledge transforms into mastery.

Most people never reach this point.

They collect information endlessly. They move from one strategy to another. They chase tools and trends. They remain in perpetual preparation. Action stays inconsistent. Progress remains unstable. Potential is never fully realized.

Mastery requires synthesis.

It requires turning many lessons into one coherent way of working and thinking.

Throughout this book, you have explored systems for organization, income, authority, automation, leadership, and resilience. These systems are interconnected. Your command center supports your workflows. Your pipelines depend on your authority. Your finances reinforce your discipline. Your leadership shapes your culture.

When these elements align, momentum becomes natural.

Early in their journeys, many builders believe mastery will arrive someday after enough learning. In reality, mastery emerges through application. Each cycle of action and reflection strengthens judgment. Each challenge increases capacity.

Olivia experienced this after years of building her education platform. At first, she followed templates and mentors closely. Over time, she modified systems based on experience. Eventually, she stopped needing external models. Principles had become internalized. Confidence stabilized. Mastery arrived quietly.

Integration also requires balance. Many beginners oscillate between obsession and disengagement. They work intensely for short periods and then burn out. Sustainable builders cultivate rhythm. They balance effort with recovery. This preserves creativity and judgment.

Technology will continue evolving. Tools will become faster and more powerful. However, the principles in this book will remain relevant. Systems thinking, ethical leadership, disciplined execution, and continuous learning transcend specific platforms.

One of the most important shifts is identity. You stop seeing yourself as someone "trying to succeed." You see yourself as a builder. A steward. A designer of systems. This identity stabilizes behavior and anchors commitment.

The path forward is not about perfection. It is about refinement. Every system will require adjustment. Every strategy will encounter limits. Every success will introduce new responsibility. Mastery is a practice.

Doubt will appear. Markets will shift. Competition will increase. During these moments, return to fundamentals. Strengthen foundations. Simplify where complexity has accumulated. Reconnect with purpose.

Legacy is created through consistent contribution. Through people helped. Through systems shared. Through standards upheld. Through integrity maintained. Over time, these form a quiet but powerful imprint.

Before closing this book, reflect on what you have learned. Identify systems to implement immediately. Choose one habit to strengthen this month. Commit to focused action.

The future belongs to those who design it.

You now have the tools. You now have the frameworks. You now have the responsibility.

What remains is execution.

With clarity.
With discipline.
With integrity.
With patience.

Your journey continues.

FINAL WORD

The Work Is Now Yours

You have reached the end of this book.

That matters.

Not because you finished reading, but because you stayed long enough to understand.

Most people look for shortcuts. They collect information the way others collect entertainment. They start with enthusiasm and abandon with excuses.

You stayed.

Now the responsibility shifts.

Nothing in these pages will change your life on its own. Knowledge does not transform. Execution does. Discipline does. Structure does.

The systems outlined here are not theories. They are frameworks for ownership.

You now understand that income is not random. It is engineered. Stability is not granted. It is constructed. Freedom is not declared. It is earned through repetition, refinement, and restraint.

There will be seasons when progress is invisible. There will be moments when doubt feels louder than confidence. There will be opportunities to return to comfort.

Build anyway.

Not aggressively.
Not impulsively.
But steadily.

The modern economy rewards leverage, clarity, and adaptability. It punishes distraction and dependency. You are no longer operating blindly within it. You now have structure.

Use it.

Choose one system and commit to it. Resist the urge to chase every idea. Refine what you start. Improve what you build. Strengthen what works.

Let others chase noise. You build signal.

One day, someone will ask how you created stability in an unstable time. They will see the outcome and assume it was sudden.

It was not sudden.

It was structured.

The difference between those who admire independence and those who achieve it is simple:

One group consumes.

The other constructs.

Decide which one you are.

LeSean Thomas

THANK YOU TO THE READER

To You, the Reader,

Thank you for choosing this book.

Thank you for investing your time, attention, and energy in your own growth.

In a world filled with distractions and shortcuts, choosing to learn, reflect, and improve is a powerful decision. It speaks to your character and your commitment to building something meaningful.

You did not pick up this book by accident.

You picked it up because you want more than temporary success.
You want stability.
You want clarity.
You want ownership.

I respect that.

My hope is that these pages help you move forward with confidence, discipline, and purpose.

Whatever stage you are in, keep building.

You are capable of more than you realize.

LeSean Thomas

LEGACY STATEMENT

This book is not about quick wins.

It is about what lasts.

It is about creating systems that outlive motivation. Building habits that outlast trends. Developing character that outlasts challenges.

My goal is not simply to teach people how to earn.

It is to help them become builders.

Builders of skills.
Builders of structure.
Builders of opportunity.
Builders of independence.

If this book helps even one person move from uncertainty to stability, from confusion to clarity, or from dependency to ownership, then it has served its purpose.

True success is not measured by attention.

It is measured by impact.

This is the legacy I seek to leave.

LeSean Thomas

The Real Message of This Book

This book is not about quick money.
It's not about shortcuts.
And it's not about hype.

It's about something far more powerful.

It's About Building Systems, Not Hustles

Most people are stuck in a cycle:

Work → Get Paid → Start Over → Repeat

That's not freedom. That's survival.

This book teaches you how to build:

Systems → Assets → Leverage → Stability

So your effort continues working even when you're not.

Real wealth is not built from constant hustle. It's built from intelligent systems.

It's About Turning Knowledge Into Income

You already know more than you think.

Your experiences. Your skills.Your lessons.

They all have value.

This book shows you how to:

- Package what you know
- Automate delivery

- Sell ethically
- Scale responsibly

So your knowledge becomes an asset — not just a memory.

It's About Using AI as a Tool — Not a Crutch

AI in this book is a productivity partner, a research assistant, a systems builder, a leverage tool.

But it is not a replacement for your thinking.

You stay in control. You make the decisions.You lead.

AI simply helps you move faster and smarter.

It's About Becoming Independent

This is the heart of everything.

Not dependent on one job.
Not dependent on one boss.
Not dependent on one platform.
Not dependent on one trend.

But capable of adapting, rebuilding, and growing — no matter what changes.

True security does not come from certainty. It comes from capability.

It's About Discipline, Integrity, and Legacy

Unlike most "make money" books, this one makes something clear:

Success without character collapses.

That's why this book emphasizes financial discipline, ethical business, long-term thinking, and a leadership mindset.

You don't just make money.

You build something that lasts. You build something you're proud of. You build a legacy.

Your Next Steps Start Now

You have finished *The AI Income Playbook.*

But finishing the book is not the goal.

Building your system is.

Reading gives you awareness. Action gives you results.

This page exists to help you turn what you've learned into real momentum.

STEP 1: Commit to a 30-Day Build Phase

For the next 30 days, make this your priority:

Build one income system.

Not five.
Not ten.
One.

Choose a simple starting point:

- A digital product
- A freelance service
- An automated workflow
- A consulting offer
- A content system

Progress beats perfection.

Write it here:

My first system will be:

STEP 2: Set a Weekly Execution Routine

Consistency is your advantage.

Each week, commit to:

- 2–3 focused work sessions
- 60–90 minutes each
- No distractions

Put them on your calendar now.

This is how builders win.

STEP 3: Build Your Command Center

If you haven't already, create your digital workspace:

- One folder for ideas
- One folder for assets
- One folder for systems
- One folder for finances

Order creates momentum.

STEP 4: Apply AI as a Partner

Use AI intentionally for:

- Planning
- Research
- Writing
- Automation
- Optimization

Not to replace thinking. To strengthen it.

Ask better questions. Expect better results.

STEP 5: Track One Metric

Choose one number to monitor weekly:

- Revenue
- Leads
- Subscribers
- Clients
- Conversions

What you measure improves.

Write it here:

My main metric is:

STEP 6: Request Your Bonus Resources

To support your journey, you can access additional tools, templates, and updates.

Visit: [Insert your website or email signup here]

Or email: [Insert your contact email here]

You will receive:

- System templates
- Checklists
- Worksheets
- Updates
- Training invites

No spam. Only tools.

YOUR COMMITMENT

You have reached the final page of this book.

Now the real work begins.

Finishing a book changes nothing.

Building does.

The ideas in these pages were never meant to inspire admiration. They were meant to be applied. They are not trends. They are not shortcuts. They are not motivation dressed as strategy.

They are systems.

And systems only matter when they are executed.

There will be no perfect moment. There will be no sudden clarity. There will be no guarantee of comfort.

You build anyway.

Not impulsively.
Not emotionally.
But deliberately.

Choose one system.

Design it.
Launch it.
Refine it.
Strengthen it.

Then repeat.

Do not chase speed. Chase structure.

Do not chase attention. Chase stability.

Over time, discipline compounds. Systems compound. Ownership compounds.

And so does freedom.

Most people will close this book and return to distraction.

A few will close this book and begin construction.

That difference is everything.

Decide who you are.

LeSean Thomas

Stop starting over. Start building.

ABOUT THE AUTHOR

LeSean Thomas is an entrepreneur and system builder focused on designing ethical, scalable, AI-powered income ecosystems. His work emphasizes structure, discipline, and long-term impact over short-term hype. Through practical systems and principled leadership, he helps individuals transform effort into lasting opportunity.

www.ingramcontent.com/pod-product-compliance
Lightning Source LLC
LaVergne TN
LVHW050923210926
848482LV00012B/513